D1299513

MacIntyre Purcell Publishing Inc.
194 Hospital Rd.
Lunenburg, Nova Scotia
B0J 2C0
(902) 640-3350

www.macintyrepurcell.com
info@macintyrepurcell.com


Printed and bound in Canada by Marquis
Design and layout: Channel Communications and Alex Hickey

Library and Archives Canada Cataloguing in Publication

De Adder, Michael, 1967-, author
     You might be from Canada if... / Michael de Adder.

ISBN 978-1-77276-063-7 (softcover)

     1. Canada--Humor.  2. National characteristics, Canadian--Humor.  3. Canadian wit and humor.  I. Title.

FC173.D43 2017          971.002'07          C2017-902032-3


MacIntyre Purcell Publishing Inc. would like to acknowledge the financial support of the Government of Canada and the Nova Scotia Department of Tourism, Culture and Heritage.

# YOU MIGHT BE FROM CANADA IF...

## BY MICHAEL DE ADDER

# FOREWORD

You must be from elsewhere if you don't LOL at this book!

Michael de Adder is the most widely distributed political cartoonist in Canada. If you are one of those bright people who actually still reads, you can't help but have seen his drawings in newspapers and other publications everywhere with his distinctive de Adder signature. Indeed, they would have jumped off the page at you, what with his hard-hitting political commentary and ready wit.

There are days – and try to understand how hard it is for a cartoonist to admit this – that I prefer Michael's sketches to my own! And I'm not alone. Michael is watched very carefully by all the other master cartoonists in the country: Gable, MacKinnon, Chapleau, Mayes and Donato – just to name a few.

There may be a reason for Michael's brightness: He might be my illegitimate son! Witness: de Adder draws very funny short people with big heads. I've been known to draw short people with big heads. Could that be because he and I are both short(ish), and have rather large heads? Hmm …

And look at the math: In 1967, Canada was 100 years old. That was the same year that I started cartooning – and that Michael was born. Just sayin'.… Furthermore, Canada is now 150 years old; I have been cartooning for 50 years; Michael de Adder is 50 years old. It all adds up! I think, so anyway. But then, I'm now 75, an age when I sometimes forget things – or make things up.

This book is part of a departure that de Adder ventured upon several books ago with his "You Must Be From …" series. Instead of this being a collection of political cartoons, these drawings are a salute to the charming foibles and eccentricities of average Canadians everywhere. Long may we live! And we all have the best of friends in Michael.

*—Terry Mosher, the cartoonist for the*
Montreal Gazette, *works under the pen name Aislin.*
*He has also published a book this year entitled*
From Trudeau to Trudeau: Aislin, Fifty Years of Cartooning.

# INTRODUCTION

You'd think it would be easy to define what it is to be Canadian. The truth of the matter is, it's very difficult to define us as one people. And the more you scratch the surface, the more difficult it becomes.

It seems at least we have location in common. "As Canadians we all live or have lived in Canada" is a true statement.

But does this mean we all live in the same place?

Canada is twice as large as the European Union.

Nobody says that living in Calais is the same as living in Prague. And obviously living in Toronto is not the same as living in Iqaluit. But Toronto has far more in common with Iqaluit than Calais has with Prague. Even with this said, Iqaluit is less concerned about transit issues than Toronto, and Toronto is less concerned about polar bears.

So how do you approach a book called *You Might Be From Canada If...* and be relevant to people in Toronto and Iqaluit at the same time?

Believe it or not, you start with hockey. Paul Henderson's goal. Most would consider that a common moment. And if you don't consider that a common moment as a Canadian, you appreciate that at least most Canadians do. But for those people who may not like hockey (there are two in Canada), on the next cartoon you try to draw something not about hockey. You draw Ernie Coombs, Terry Fox, then polar bears. And you do your best to be inclusive.

We are a patchwork of experiences. Some common and others less common. This book is like small pieces of cloth I've sewn together. And hopefully by the time you're done, you'll step back and see a quilt; a quilt that resembles Canada.

• • •

This book started when I did the first book in the *You Might* series called *You Might Be From Nova Scotia If...* There was no plan to do *You Might Be From Canada If...* but in making my list for the Nova Scotia book, I kept asking myself if the items on my list could be classified as a Nova Scotian experience or more of a general Canadian experience.

The same thing happened when I did *You Might Be From New Brunswick If...* and then *You Might Be From Newfoundland and Labrador If...*

My list of things Canadian just kept growing after each book I drew.

So the list of people I'm thanking in this book are people who have helped on previous books as well.

I'd like to thank Meredith MacKinlay who has helped on my last four books. Every book has been made better by her suggestions, encouragement, design experience and copy editing.

My brothers, Paul De Adder and David De Adder were great sounding boards and weren't afraid to tell me when I sucked. In fact they took great joy in telling me I sucked. I'd like to thank Trudy De Adder for putting up with David De Adder.

All helped with the book.

I'd like to thank my mother, Marilyn, for being my mother. It couldn't be easy with three boys, and she always did her very best.

I'd like to thank the post ball hockey "Podcast" composed of myself, Dan Frid and Geoff Brown. I put Podcast in quotations because it's not a real podcast.

I'd like to thank Jenny Gray for putting up with the "Podcast" and calling it the "Podcast" even though she knows it's just three guys saying dumb things while she rolls her eyes.

I'd like to thank artist Dawn Mockler for looking at my online portfolio and sharing thoughts and recommendations.

And thanks to Terry Mosher for being an inspiration, a friend and for his kind words.

Since *You Might Be From Nova Scotia If...* in 2012, dozens of other people helped with other books, and directly or indirectly with this book. I'd like to repeat my thanks to Greg Little, Shaune MacKinlay, Julian Marchant, Joanne Marchant, Erin Dwyer, Jerry West, Kim Lake, Edna Singer, David Rodenhiser, Marla Cranston, Gisele Mcknight, John MacIntyre and his beer buddies.

Finally, I'd like to thank the most important people in my life. I'd like to thank Gail yet again for taking up the slack, and Meaghan and Bridget for all the times I had to spend working on this book. We have a vacation coming and I have a lot of soccer and ringette games to make up. I love you all.

FOR PAUL

# YOU MIGHT BE FROM CANADA IF...

YOU RAKE AND BAG YOUR NATIONAL SYMBOL EVERY FALL.

IT'S NOT YOUR 150TH BIRTHDAY.

YOU BUY HOMO MILK IN BAGS.

1. SOME GUY
2. SOME GUY
3. SOME GUY
4. SOME GUY
5. SOME GUY
6. JOHN A MACDONALD
7. SOME GUY
8. SOME GUY
9. SOME GUY
10. SOME GUY
11. SOME GUY
12. SOME GUY
13. SOME GUY
14. SOME GUY
15. SOME GUY
16. SOME GUY
17. SOME GUY
18. SOME GUY
19. SOME GUY
20. SOME GUY
21. SOME GUY
22. SOME GUY
23. SOME GUY
24. SOME GUY
25. SOME GUY
26. SOME GUY
27. SOME GUY
28. SOME GUY
29. SOME GUY
30. SOME GUY
31. SOME GUY
32. SOME GUY
33. SOME GUY
34. SOME GUY
35. SOME GUY
36. SOME GUY
37. SOME GUY

YOU CAN NAME ONLY ONE OF THE ORIGINAL FATHERS OF CONFEDERATION...

LORD STANLEY'S CUP

GREY CUP

...BUT YOU CAN NAME TWO GOVERNORS GENERAL.

YOU KNOW THE GOAL HEARD AROUND THE WORLD.

YOU STILL CAN'T BELIEVE GRETZKY GOT TRADED.

YOU ARE ENDLESSLY PROUD THAT JACKIE ROBINSON
STARTED HIS CAREER IN CANADA.

YOU REMEMBER THE DAY AN AMERICAN
FROM OKLAHOMA BECAME A CANADIAN HERO.

YOU CAN NAME EVERYBODY ON THIS CURRENCY.

YOU HAVE A HARD TIME NAMING EVERYBODY ON THIS CURRENCY.

EVERYTHING YOU KNOW ABOUT CANADIAN NATURE YOU LEARNED FROM COMMERCIALS.

EVERYTHING YOU KNOW ABOUT CANADIAN HISTORY YOU LEARNED FROM COMMERCIALS.

YOU KEEP A HUGE WAD OF CASH LYING AROUND.

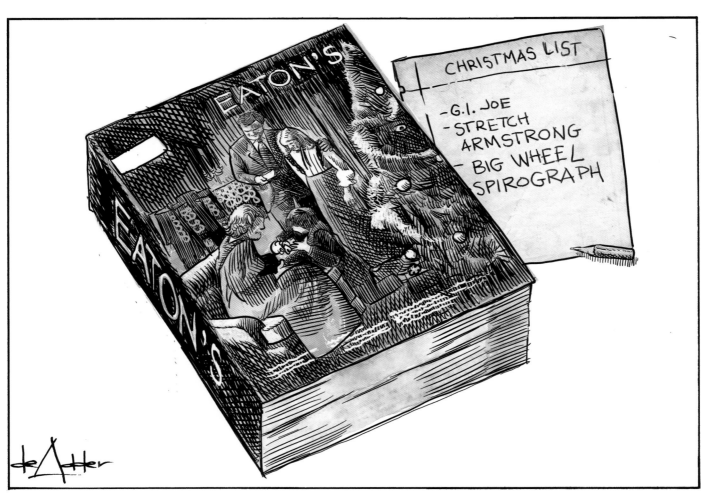

YOU MADE YOUR CHRISTMAS LIST USING
THE EATON'S FALL AND WINTER CATALOGUE.

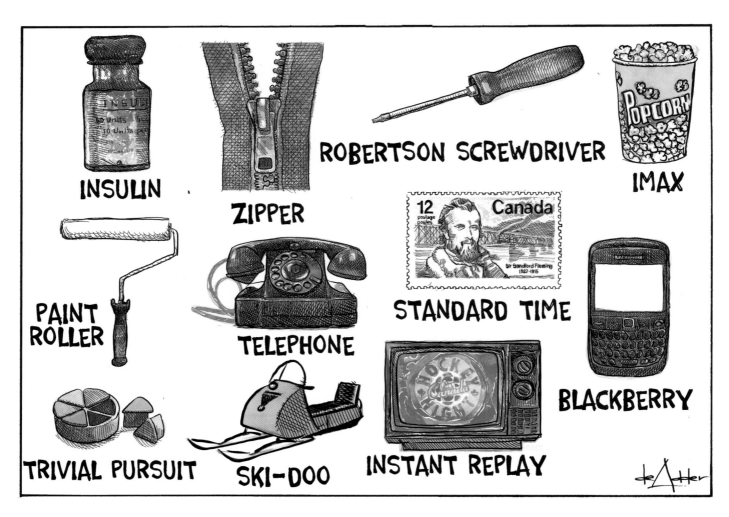

YOUR INVENTIONS CHANGED THE MODERN WORLD.

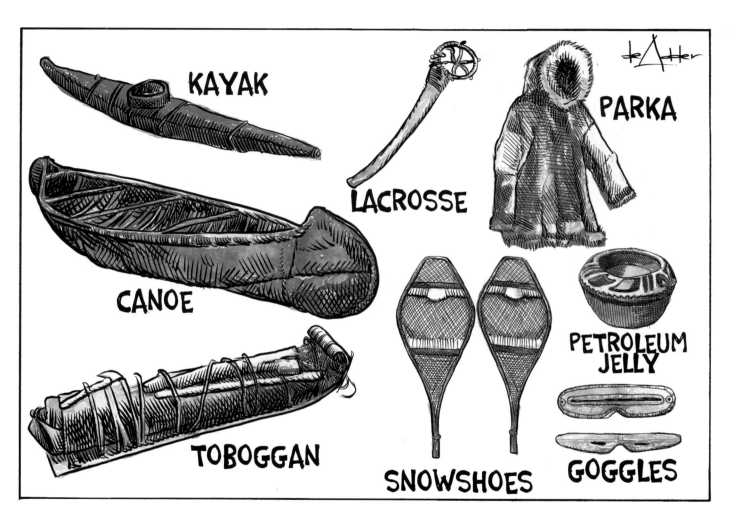

YOUR INVENTIONS CHANGED THE OLD WORLD.

CHESTERFIELD

DOUBLE DOUBLE

C...EH n...EH d...EH
EH

WASHROOM

TOQUE

CHINOOK

LINEUP

GITCH

CANADIAN TUXEDO

FREEZIE

ROTTEN RONNIE'S

TIN

YOU UNDERSTAND THESE WORDS.

YOU'RE SORRY FOR EVERYTHING.

YOU THINK MIXING CLAM JUICE AND TOMATO JUICE IS A GOOD IDEA.

THIS IS YOUR EXERCISE EQUIPMENT.

YOU KNOW SUPERMAN WAS CO-INVENTED BY A CANADIAN.

WOLVERINE          DEADPOOL          CAPTAIN
                                     CANUCK

YOU KNOW THE SUPERHEROES BORN IN CANADA.

YOU KNOW ALL YOUR HOCKEY HEROES BY THEIR FIRST NAME.

YOU EAT CHOCOLATE BARS, NOT CANDY BARS.

YOUR HEROES DON'T ALWAYS FINISH.

A CONCERT MADE YOU TEAR UP.

YOU ONLY NEED THREE DOWNS.

YOU KNOW THE THRILL OF VICTORY
AND THE AGONY OF DEFEAT.

YOU HOPE THE HEATER MELTS THE ICE OFF
YOUR WINDSHIELD BEFORE THE COPS SEE YOU.

YOU PLUG IN YOUR CAR AND IT'S NOT ELECTRIC.

YOUR ARTISTS TRAVEL IN PACKS.

EMILY CARR

YOU THINK THE GROUP OF SEVEN COULD
HAVE BEEN CALLED THE GROUP OF EIGHT.

YOU EITHER LOVE RUSH WITH A PASSION
OR HATE RUSH WITH A PASSION.

WHEN YOU LOOK AT ALEX TREBEK, YOU CAN'T
HELP BUT THINK SOMETHING IS MISSING.

BEN AFFLECK          KEN TAYLOR

YOU KNOW BATMAN DIDN'T SAVE THE
AMERICAN HOSTAGES IN IRAN, A CANADIAN DID.

YOU LIKE TO TELL AMERICANS THAT BASKETBALL WAS INVENTED BY A CANADIAN.

IT'S IMPOSSIBLE TO DRESS FOR THE WEATHER.

YOUR MOTHER TIED YOUR MITTENS TOGETHER.

YOU SLYLY GET AROUND TAKING THE LORD'S NAME IN VAIN.

A CHILDREN'S BOOK MADE YOU CRY LIKE A BABY.

YOU MISS STUBBIES.

YOU CONSIDER THESE BOTTLED WATER.

YOU FIND THESE PLACE NAMES QUITE NORMAL.

YOUR DIET IS ALL OVER THE MAP.

YOU FOUND THE PERFECT ITEM ONLINE, BUT THEY DON'T DELIVER TO CANADA.

THAT VIDEO IS UNAVAILABLE IN YOUR COUNTRY.

YOU CAN GAUGE THE SUCCESS OF YOUR HOUSE PARTY
BY THE SIZE OF THE PILE OF BOOTS AT THE DOOR.

YOU HAVE A PILE OF GLOVES AND MITTS, ALL SEEMINGLY FOR THE SAME HAND.

YOU KNOW THE CANADA GOOSE IS THE ASSHOLE
OF THE BIRD FAMILY.

CANADA GEESE

DUCKS

SANDPIPERS

SNOW BIRDS

YOU FLY SOUTH FOR THE WINTER.

YOU'VE PRAYED FOR A SNOW DAY.

THE ROMPER ROOM WOMAN NEVER SAID YOUR NAME.

YOU DON'T THINK THE WAR OF 1812 WAS A DRAW.

YOUR PAUL REVERE WAS LAURA SECORD.

YOU CAN MOUTH THE WORDS TO "O CANADA"
IN BOTH OFFICIAL LANGUAGES.

YOU WELCOME HOME YOUR FALLEN SOLDIERS
IN THE MOST CANADIAN OF WAYS.

CANADA IS YOUR NEW HOME.

YOUR TEEN DRAMA IS FULL OF DRAMA.

DRAKE WILL ALWAYS BE JIMMY BROOKS.

YOU'RE NOT SURE WHY, BUT FRIES ALWAYS TASTE BETTER AT THE RINK.

YOU SAY ZED, NOT ZEE.

THERE'S EVIDENCE YOU WERE HERE.

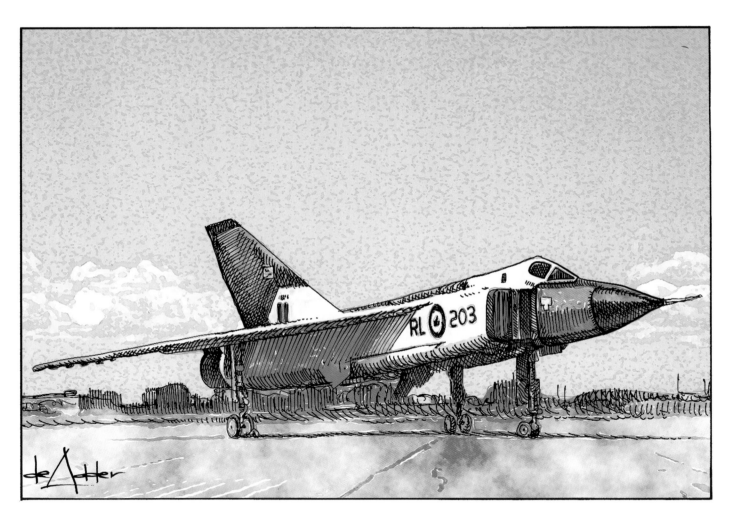

YOU'RE STILL NOT SURE WHAT HAPPENED TO THE AVRO ARROW.

YOU REMEMBER THE BEACHCOMBERS.

YOU KNOW CANADIANS AREN'T THE ONLY ONES
OBSESSED WITH ANNE OF GREEN GABLES.

YOU'VE HAD A WOMAN AS YOUR HEAD OF STATE
FOR THE PAST 65 YEARS.

LOUIS RIEL IS STILL CONTROVERSIAL.

THANKSGIVING IS A MONTH EARLIER WITHOUT
THE PILGRIMS OR THE FOOTBALL.

YOU GO INTO A SPORTS BAR AND CURLING IS ON.

YOU ALREADY GOT BEER AND POUTINE ON THIS BOOK.

YOU'VE DONE THIS ONLY ONCE.

# RODENTS

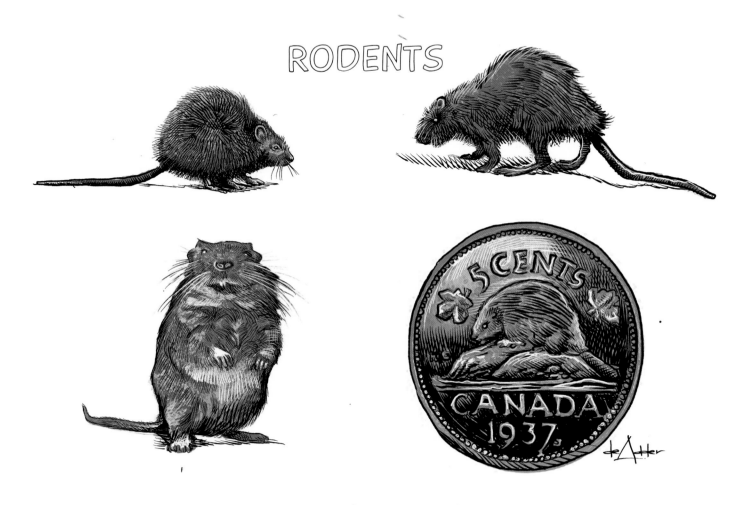

**YOUR NATIONAL SYMBOL IS A RODENT.**

AMERICANS THINK YOU SAY "A-BOOT" BUT
YOU KNOW YOU SAY "A-BOAT."

YOU HAVE YOUR OWN WAY OF MAKING KD.

YOU'RE SHOCKED THAT THESE FLAVOURS ONLY EXIST IN CANADA.

YOU'VE PLAYED AGAIN AND AGAIN AND AGAIN.

YOU HAVE A HUGE POCKETFUL OF COINS.

YOUR WALLET WAS RETURNED TO YOU WITH THE MONEY STILL IN IT.

YOUR COUNTRY HUNG ON BY A THREAD.

YOU KNOW SANTA CLAUS IS A PERMANENT RESIDENT OF CANADA.

YOU KNOW THE RCMP MUSICAL RIDE ISN'T A TRIP
TO THE DRUNK TANK WITH THE RADIO ON.

YOU SEE NOTHING WRONG WITH EATING BEAVERTAILS.

YOU WERE ON A ONE-ON-ONE AND SOMEBODY YELLED **CAR!**

YOU THINK YOUR HOLIDAY IS NAMED MAY TWO-FOUR
BECAUSE YOU ALWAYS BUY A TWO-FOUR.

THIS IS CANADIAN FASHION WEEK.

YOU'VE PLAYED "NAME THAT ROADKILL."

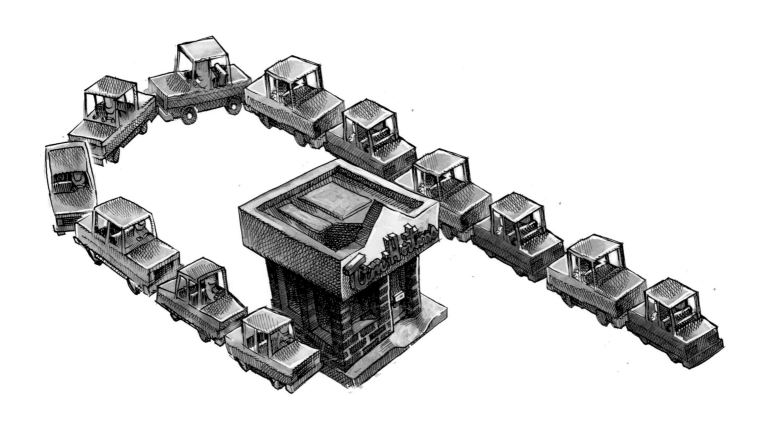

YOU HATE WAITING IN LINE AT THE BANK,
BUT WILL WAIT ALL DAY FOR A COFFEE.

IT'S EASY TO SPOT OTHER CANADIANS WHEN TRAVELLING.

THE SUMMER SEASON IS TOO SHORT, BUT BBQ SEASON NEVER ENDS.

TO CHILL YOUR BEER, YOU ONLY NEED
TO PUT THEM ON THE DECK.

YOU KNOW THE BEST GAME YOU CAN PLAY.

YOU'VE HAD A LONG WAIT FOR A STANLEY CUP WIN.

YOUR FEMALE ATHLETES BRING HOME THE HARDWARE.

WE DON'T ALWAYS GET ALONG.

YOU BELIEVE IN TRUTH AND RECONCILIATION.

IT'S SO COLD YOUR NOSTRILS HAVE FROZEN TOGETHER.

IN A SNOW STORM YOU REDUCE YOUR SPEED
TO THE POSTED SPEED LIMIT.

YOU DIDN'T VISIT MR. ROGERS' NEIGHBOURHOOD, YOU VISITED
CASEY AND FINNEGAN'S TREEHOUSE.

YOU WANTED A BIGGER CHAIR FOR TWO TO CURL UP IN.

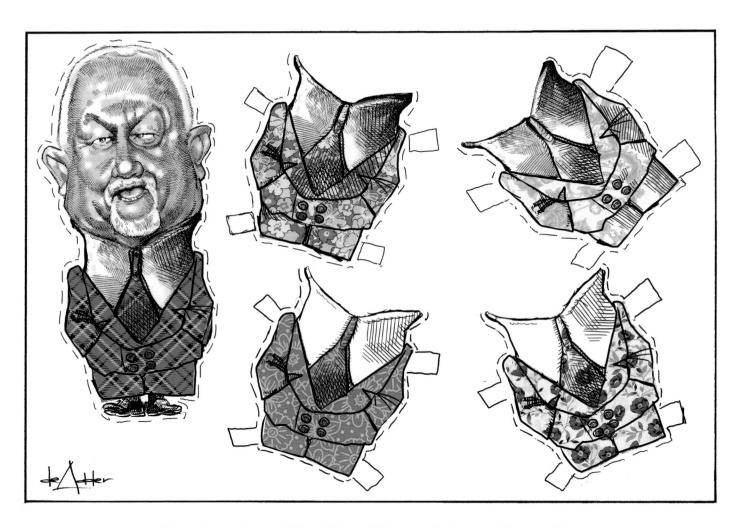

LOVE HIM OR HATE HIM, YOU CAN'T IGNORE DON CHERRY.

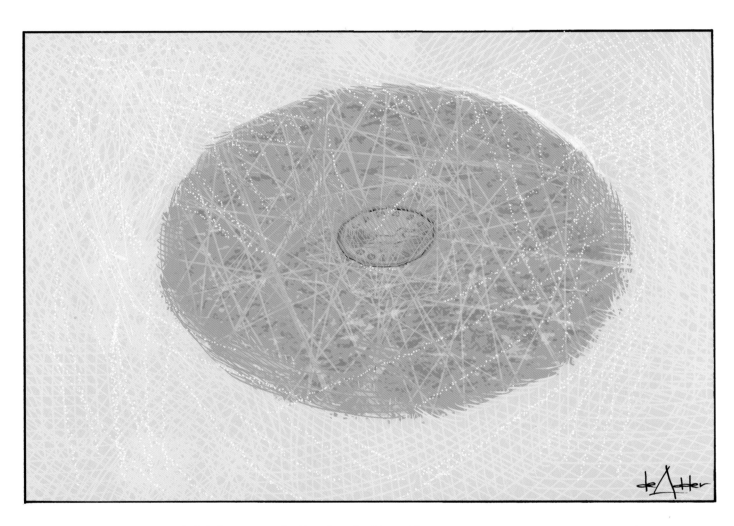

YOU KNOW WHY THERE'S A LOONIE IN THE HOCKEY HALL OF FAME.

THESE ROAD SIGNS SEEM PERFECTLY NORMAL.

YOU HAVE YOUR OWN CANADIANISMS FOR LIQUOR.

YOU DROPPED EVERYTHING TO GO FIGHT THE NAZIS.

YOU'RE CONSTANTLY REMINDED THAT NEWFOUNDLAND
HAS ITS OWN TIME ZONE.

LASSIE DIDN'T COME TO THE RESCUE.

YOU HAD YOUR OWN GAME SHOWS.

YOU'RE MAD WHEN THE PLOW DOESN'T SHOW UP.

YOU'RE MAD WHEN THE PLOW DOES SHOW UP.

YOU REMEMBER WHEN YOUPI WAS AN EXPO.

YOU FIND LE BONHOMME A LITTLE SCARY.

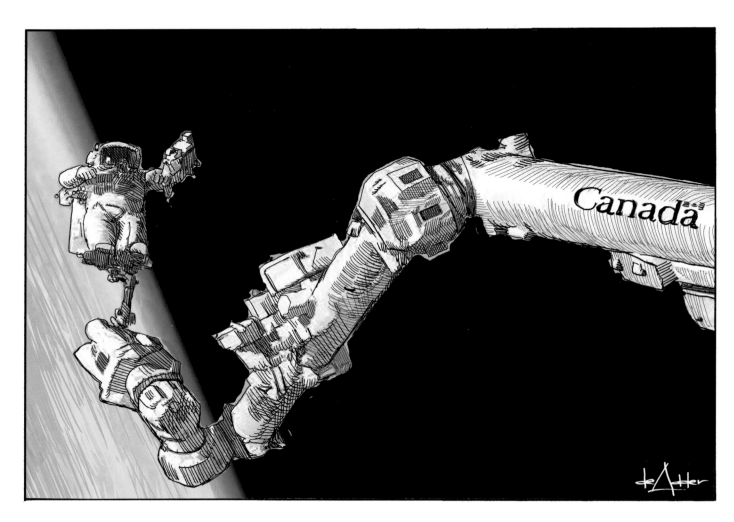

YOU CALL THE ROBOTIC ARM BY ITS REAL NAME, THE CANADARM.

YOU'RE A SPACE EXPLORER.

YOU'RE A COMEDIAN.

YOU'RE A MUSICIAN.

YOU SUFFERED DEFEAT ON THE BEACHES OF DIEPPE ...

... BUT THAT DIDN'T STOP YOU FROM VICTORY ON THE BEACHES OF NORMANDY.

YOU ARE REMINDED EVERY REMEMBRANCE DAY THAT
A CANADIAN WROTE "IN FLANDERS FIELDS."

# END NOTES

Page 9: Maple Leaf

Page 10: When exactly First Nations people settled in North America is widely disputed. I went with the number which seemed to be the most accurate – 13,500 years ago. Many numbers could have been used. I had to pick one. What is more certain that in 1867 Canada comprised just Nova Scotia, New Brunswick, Ontario and Quebec.

Page 11: Homo milk stands for homogenized milk.

Page 12: A lot of people can name more than one Father of Confederation. For example, Joseph Howe [#34] is famous in Nova Scotia even to this day. But for the sake of a joke, most people only recognize John A. MacDonald, the Prime Minister of the day.

Page 14: Canada–USSR Series was an eight-game series of ice hockey between the Soviet Union and Canada, held in September, 1972. This is a drawing of Frank Lennon's famous photograph of Paul Henderson at the moment he scored the winning goal that won the series.

Page 17: 1993 World Series Joe Carter's walk-off home run to end the series.

Page 30: Superman was created by writer Jerry Siegel and artist Joe Shuster. Joe Shuster was Canadian-born.

Page 34: Terry Fox

Page 35: The Tragically Hip's lead singer, Gord Downie.

Page 37: Ben Johnson

Page 40: The Group of Seven were Franklin Carmichael, Lawren Harris, A. Y. Jackson, Frank Johnston, Arthur Lismer, J. E. H. MacDonald, and Frederick Varley.

Page 41: Arguably, many say Emily Carr would have been in the Group of Seven if she wasn't a woman.

Page 44: In the 2012 Oscar-winning movie, Argo, directed by Ben Affleck, Americans were depicted saving the American hostages in Iran. Canadian Ambassador Ken Taylor in fact hid the Americans and saved the hostages with CIA help.

Page 45: Canadian James Naismith invented the game of basketball.

Page 53: For the sake of making the image visually pleasing, the placement of all the food is not geographically accurate. Some are close, others are way off. It's just a visual representation.

Page 58: This cartoon is accurate. The Canada Goose is a known asshole.

Page 62: The intent of the War of 1812 was the invasion of Canada. Canada, with Britain, stopped the American invasion, winning the War of 1812, and delivering the Americans their first loss in history.

Page 63: Laura Secord is known for having walked 32 km out of American-occupied territory to warn British forces of an impending American attack during the War of 1812.

Page 66: Highway of Heroes.

Page 67: While many countries turned Syrian refugees away, Canada bucked the trend and welcomed thousands as new Canadian citizens.

Page 73: Avro Arrow was a technologically advanced delta-winged interceptor aircraft abruptly cancelled on February 20, 1959 by the Canadian government. Much controversy and mystery still surround the project.

Page 75: Anne of Green Gables is huge in Japan after it was translated secretly by Hanako Muraoka during WWII and became a part of the school curriculum by 1952.

Page 85: Ketchup, All Dressed and Dill Pickle are flavours popular only in Canada.

Page 94: May 2-4 Weekend is a three-day weekend encompassing Victoria Day, which is a Canadian statutory holiday celebrated on the Monday preceding May 25. In Quebec this holiday is called National Patriots' Day (Journée nationale des patriotes).

Page 101: The best game you can play is the good ol' hockey game. – Stompin' Tom Connors

Page 102: The last time before the completion of this book that the Leafs won the Stanley Cup was 1967, the month before I was born. At the moment, as I write this, the Leafs are in the playoffs. As you read this, you will know the outcome.

Page 103: Canadian women won 72% of Canada's medals, including the first 12, at the Rio Olympics, and 16 in total.

Page 104: The Oka Crisis was a land dispute between a group of Mohawk people and the town of Oka, Quebec, which occurred in 1990.

Page 105: The Truth and Reconciliation Commission of Canada was a Canadian response to the abuse inflicted on Indigenous peoples through the residential school system.

Page 108: Mr. Dressup was a children's television series. [1967-1996]

Page 109: The Friendly Giant was a children's television series. [1958-1985]

Page 111: Trent Evans secretly placed a loonie at centre ice at the 2002 Salt Lake Winter Olympics as a good luck charm for Team Canada.

Page 116: The Littlest Hobo is a television series based upon a film of the same name.

Page 117: Front Page Challenge [1957-1995]

Page 123: Space explorers – Bjarni Tryggvason, Julie Payette, Chris Hadfield, Marc Garneau, Steve MacLean, Roberta Bondar, Dave Williams, Robert Thirsk, Montgomery Scott and James T. Kirk.

Page 124: [6th Row] Dave Broadfoot, Roger Abbott, Olivier Guimond, Gilles Latulippe, Yvon Deschamps, Claude Blanchard, Claude Meunier, Luba Goy, Don Ferguson [5th Row] Cathy Jones, Rick Mercer, Andrea Martin, Mark Critch, Mary Walsh, Mike Smith, John Paul Tremblay, Robb Wells [4th Row] Norm Macdonald, Johnny Wayne, Frank Shuster, Lorne Michaels, Phil Hartman, Catherine O'Hara, Dave Thomas, Rick Moranis, Dave Foley [3rd Row] Michael Cera, Will Arnett, Ellen Page, Rich Little, Tommy Chong, Colin Mochrie, Ivan Reitman, Scott Thompson, Kevin McDonald [2nd Row] Jason Reitman, Dan Aykroyd, Samantha Bee, Michael J Fox, Mike Myers, Seth Rogen, Jay Baruchel, Tom Green, Mark McKinney [1st Row] Martin Short, Jim Carrey, Shaun Majumder, Leslie Nielsen, Russell Peters, John Candy, Eugene Levy, Bruce McCulloch

Page 125: [6th Row] Serge Fiori [Harmonium], Sarah Harmer, Stompin' Tom Connors, Tom Cochrane, Chris Murphy [Sloan], Joel Plaskett, Measha Brueggergosman, Russell Braun [5th Row] Anne Murray, Buffy Sainte-Marie, Robbie Robertson, Glenn Gould, Diana Krall, Celine Dion, Chantal Kreviazuk, Daniel Lanois [4th Row] Avril Lavigne, Paul Anka, The Weeknd, Tegan Rain Quin, Sara Keirsten Quin, Kaytranada, Jeff Healey, Carly Rae Jepsen, Jann Arden [3rd Row] Richard Margison, Rufus Wainwright, Geddy Lee [Rush], Neil Peart [Rush], Raine Maida [Our Lady Peace], Chad Kroeger [Nickelback], Oscar Peterson, Bruce Cockburn [2nd Row] Leonard Cohen, Ed Robertson [Barenaked Ladies], Win Butler [Arcade Fire], Gordon Lightfoot, Burton Cummings [The Guess Who], Randy Bachman [The Guess Who & Bachman Turner Overdrive], Leslie Feist, Jim Cuddy [Blue Rodeo], k.d. lang [1st Row] Neil Young, Bryan Adams, Drake, Gord Downie [Tragically Hip], Joni Mitchell, Alanis Morissette, Justin Bieber, Sarah McLachlan, Shania Twain

Page 126: The Dieppe Raid, August 19th, 1942

Page 127: June 6th, 1944, D-Day [North Shore Regiment depicted.]

Page 128: Lieutenant-Colonel John McCrae. He was inspired to write it on May 3, 1915.

# TRAGICALLY HIP LYRICS

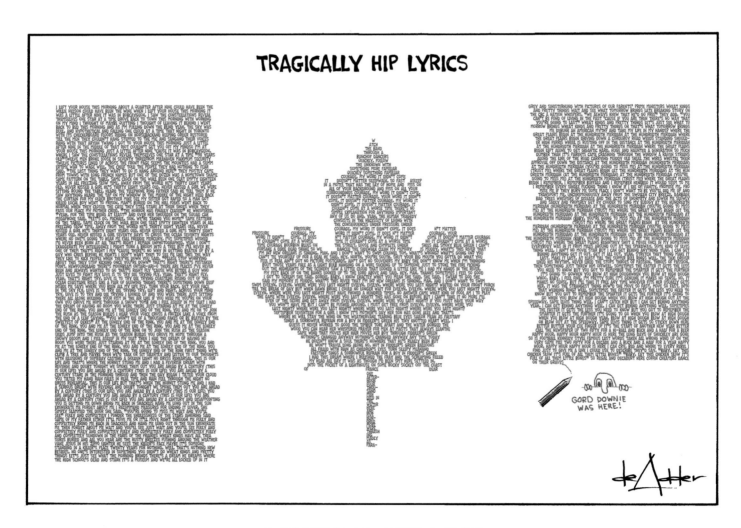

DEDICATED TO GORD DOWNIE